INTRODUCTION

Since it was introduced to service about a decade ago, the Jaguar has proven itself as a highly potent attack aircraft, specialising in low-level, single-pass, high-speed sorties in support of ground forces. It is numerically the most important strike plane currently equipping the Royal Air Force, although it performs in a role for which it typically was not at first envisaged; it has been the subject of constant development since the design was first realised (although some proposed refinements have been abandoned); and it is still in production for overseas customers.

The Jaguar is essentially a French design, but its present capabilities are due in major part to British influence, brought about when the original Breguet Br.121 was selected as the basis for a pioneering Anglo-French collaborative military aircraft project in the mid-1960s. At about this time, both the Royal Air Force and *L'Armée de l'Air* (French Air Force) had a requirement for a new advanced trainer with a secondary role as a strike aircraft. Each air force's needs differed in two respects, however: the French wanted service entry by 1970, whereas the RAF's Hunters and Gnats would need replacing by about 1975; and the Br.121's speed, a maximum just in excess of Mach 1, was less than that called for by the British proposals.

JOINT MANUFACTURE

Agreement between the two countries was reached in May 1965, the original Br.121 design being modified to permit more advanced and more comprehensive navigation/attack systems to be incorporated, a thinner wing, and more powerful engines. As a corollary, it was expected that the English Electric P.45, one of the all-British contenders for AST.362, as the Hunter/Gnat replacement requirement was designated, would serve as the basis for a complementary programme, the AFVG (Anglo-French Variable-Geometry) combat aircraft.

The agreement originally envisaged that each country would receive 150 Jaguars, the RAF variant designated 'B' (*biplace*) and *L'Armée de l'Air* versions 'A' (*appui*) and 'E' (*école*). However, British procurement plans were rapidly revised in the light of major aircraft project cancellations in 1965 (TSR.2, P.1154 and, indeed, the AFVG), and a new single seat variant, 'S' (= strike), was formulated. At the same time, the order was increased to 200 aircraft, comprising 90 'S' and 110 'B', a ratio dramatically reappraised in 1970 and finalised at 165/35; this effectively ended the prospect of the Jaguar superseding the Gnat and Hunter as an advanced trainer in the requisite numbers, and a new indigenous aircraft,

Below: One of the two French-configured Jaguar 'A' prototypes, showing the original splitter-type intakes. Other pre-production features evident here are the faired-over cannon, double-yoke nosewheel leg, early-type forward nosewheel door and absence of ventral fins. *Breguet-Aviation*

Above: The Jaguar 'E' was closest to the original Br.121 design and formed the basis from which other variants were developed. This is E-02, with ventral fins added but still retaining the early intakes; note, too, the 'short' fin, heightened in production aircraft in order to improve stability. *Avions Marcel Dassault-Breguet Aviation*
Left: An abortive Jaguar programme was the 'M' naval variant, only one example (M-05) of which was built. The principal differences concerned the undercarriage, which was strengthened and reconfigured, with twin nosewheels and single main wheels; other changes included a stronger arrester hook and a laser rangefinder below the nose. *British Aerospace*

the HS.1182 (later named Hawk – see AEROGUIDE 1) was rapidly developed to fulfil this role. A fifth Jaguar variant, 'M' (*marine*) had also been added to the programme by this time, a carrier-compatible machine designed to re-equip *Aéronavale* strike squadrons.

The Anglo-French production agreement set up a special controlling company, SEPECAT, and split the manufacture of the airframe equally between the two countries, the one-piece wing, the tail assembly and the rear fuselage being produced by BAC (British Aircraft Corporation – now part of BAe) and the forward and centre fuselage and the undercarriage being French responsibility. The powerplant, based on the RB.172 (already earmarked for the Br.121) was also produced jointly, between Rolls-Royce and Turboméca, as the Adour 102. A total of eight prototypes – 2 'E', 2 'A', 1 'M', 2 'S' and 1 'B' – were assembled prior to full production, the first of these, E-01, flying in September 1968. In June 1973 the first French Jaguar squadron was formed.

RAF ROLES

By spring 1974 the first front-line RAF Jaguar squadron, No 54, was operating from Coltishall, a Jaguar Conversion Team having been formed some six months previously at Lossiemouth. There have been eight Royal Air Force Jaguar squadrons, plus No 226 OCU at Lossiemouth: five of these were assigned to RAF Germany, along the NATO front line – Nos 14, 17, 20 and 31 at RAF Bruggen, together with No 2 Squadron (Laarbrüch) which operates in the reconnaissance role – and three, Nos 6, 41 (recce) and 54 Squadrons, to No 38 Group, the UK-based 'rapid reinforcement' unit whose Jaguars are based at Coltishall. Single-seat ('S') aircraft are designated GR Mk 1 and the 'B' two-seaters T Mk 2. Specifically, the roles of the aircraft are interdiction; tactical close support of ground forces; 'counterair' (attack projected against enemy aircraft on the ground); tactical reconnaissance (achieved by means of the BAe-designed underfuselage pod); and type conversion training (using the two-seater variant).

Left: Ground crew prepare for towing an RAF Jaguar GR Mk 1 (No 41 Squadron) at Coltishall, July 1982. GR1s were developed from the British Jaguar 'S', one of the most obvious modifications of which was the redesigned nose housing the Laser Ranger and Marked Target Seeker (LRMTS), giving RAF single-seaters (and, indeed, the standard export versions) their characteristic blunt profile forward. Jaguars currently equip eight Royal Air Force squadrons, plus an Operational Conversion Unit. Squadron complement varies, but 13 single-seaters plus a T Mk 2 is typical.

JAGUAR INTERNATIONAL

Promoting the Jaguar to overseas customers is a concern more of BAe than of its French partner, and the aircraft is currently in service with the air forces of Ecuador, the Sultan of Oman, and India. The export airframes are in essence similar to that of the RAF GR Mk 1 though have the improved Adour 804 (equivalent to the 104 retrofitted to RAF machines) and provision for air-to-air missiles; some Indian aircraft are expected to complete with the Agave nose radar in place of the ranger/target seeker to optimise the Jaguar for the anti-shipping role ('Maritime Jaguar'). It was reported in mid-1983 that Nigeria is also buying Jaguar Internationals and that Chile may acquire some ex-RAF machines.

Developments continue, particularly in respect of fly-by-wire and the fitting of Low-Light Television (LLTV) for night attack. Wing strengthening of RAF Jaguars is scheduled, in order to maximise fatigue life into the 1990s, by which time those aircraft serving in Germany are due to be replaced by Tornados (see Aeroguide 4); improved avionics in the shape of the Ferranti FIN 1064 inertial navigation system will provide even greater strike accuracy; modern ECM fits are in prospect; and the variety of stores capable of being carried by the Jaguar is constantly being widened. Moving with the times, the aircraft will doubtless provide over a quarter of a century of first-class service.

Above: In 1974 the Sultan of Oman's Air Force ordered a dozen Jaguars; two of these were two-seaters (an example is shown). A repeat order was forthcoming in mid-1980, for ten more single-seaters and a pair of trainers. *British Aerospace*

Left: The most numerically significant Jaguar export order to date has been that placed by India, for some 100 aircraft. The first batch were ex-RAF machines, a second batch was built to order by BAe, and the third was licence-produced by Hindustan Aeronautics. *British Aerospace*

Below: The second Jaguar produced for Ecuador; the paint scheme is Dark Sea Grey/Dark Green/Light Aircraft Grey. *British Aerospace.*

AIRFRAME

Below: Forward fuselage of No 54 Squadron Jaguar GR Mk 1 with inflight-refuelling probe extended; the deployment cycle is not quite complete since the lower (horizontal) door is not fully closed. Body of probe is zinc chromate finish.
Bottom: Extended forward fuselage of a T Mk 2, showing repositioned nose sensors. Forward screen and canopy are identical to that on the single-seater, but inflight refuelling is not available.
Opposite page, top: GR Mk 1 nose, showing panels for access to the LRMTS and avionics bays. Prominent fitting along upper contours is a total-pressure probe.
Opposite page, middle left: Close-up of Ferranti laser ranger and characteristic 'windows'; sealing strips around glazing are reddish-brown.
Opposite page, middle right: Interior of inflight-refuelling probe bay.
Opposite page, bottom: Port side of GR1 forward fuselage, showing cooling intake; note also matt black anti-glare panel above.

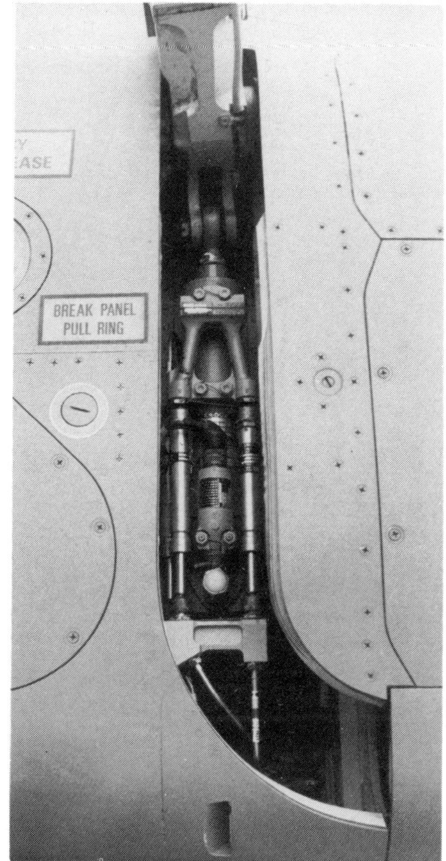
EASE
BREAK PANEL
PULL RING

Above: Top view of forward fuselage of Jaguar T Mk 2, showing walkway markings above main intake. The prominent duct behind the cockpit serves as an intake for cabin air conditioning and an outlet for the secondary heat exchanger; atop it are twin VHF homing antennas, yellowish-buff with black protective strips along their leading edges. Note the slightly differing designs of the two crew boarding ladders.

Right: Port main intake, GR Mk 1, showing weathering around this particular example and the inboard 'spacer'. T Mk 2 is similar.

Opposite page, top: Jaguar's subtle contours in the region of the intakes are highlighted in this view of a No 41 Sqn machine; the slight denting along the outer intake rim is non-standard! The photo was taken in July 1982; since then the squadron insignia have been brightened up considerably – see colour profile on the back cover of this booklet for details. The two auxiliary intake doors along the trunking are spring-loaded and are closed when the aircraft is parked. The warning notice forward of the intake is white with red lettering.

Opposite page, bottom: Starboard fuselage detail of a No 54 Sqn Jaguar GR Mk 1, mid-1982. Note paint chipping around removable panelling and on screwheads.

DANGER
AIR INTAKE
KEEP CLEAR
XII

Opposite page, top: Port rear fuselage of GR Mk 1 XZ359/'M', No 41 Sqn, July 1982, showing also typical flap angles of a Jaguar at rest. Ventral fins have black leading-edge strips.

Opposite page, bottom: Well-weathered starboard rear fuselage of a No 54 Sqn GR Mk 1 (XX727/'GJ'). Fire access panels have red rectangular surrounds; flap incidence stripe (top right) is yellow.

Above: Interior of port airbrake – general finish is the same as that for the adjacent external airframe.

Left: Detail of starboard airbrake, showing perforations and markings. Note that the bay also houses the refuelling point; the cap for the pipe is just visible.

Below left: The Jaguar's airbrakes are frequently to be seen open whilst the aircraft are on the ground, but this is not always the case, as this photo shows. The symbols are the same as those in the previous picture, but rearranged.

Below right: Jaguar's ground power attachment point (see also page 29).

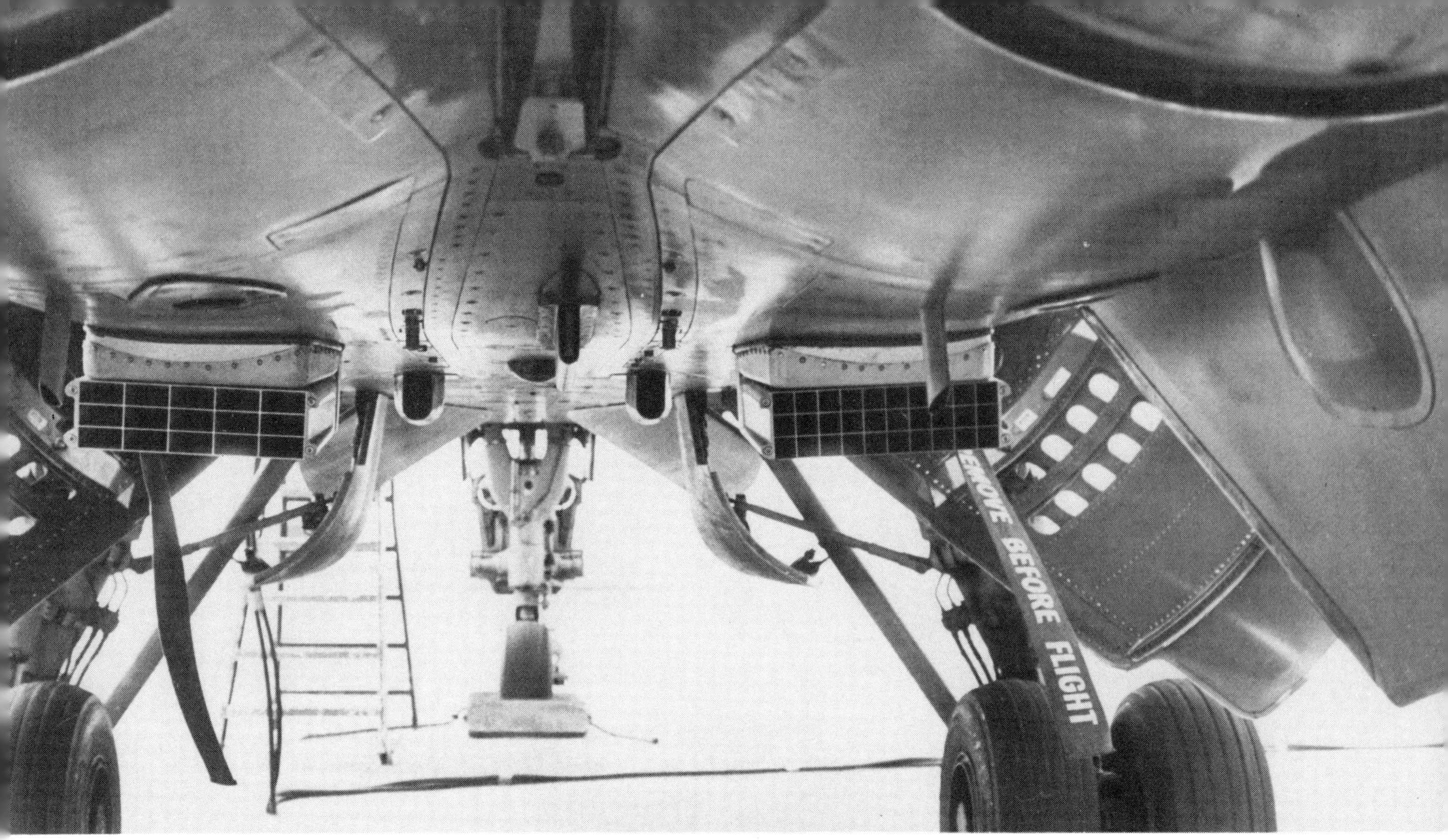

REMOVE BEFORE FLIGHT

SAFETY PIN
REMOVE

Opposite page, top: Underside view of Jaguar GR Mk 1 XZ400/'GP'; on 3 June 1983, when this photograph was taken, this aircraft had just been fitted with chaff (port) and flare (starboard) chutes for experimental purposes.
Opposite page, middle: Close-up of XZ400's flare chute; finish is natural metal. Note 'Remove Before Flight' tags (red with white lettering).

Opposite page, bottom: Business end of a Jaguar's arrester hook, unpainted.
Above: Rear fuselage of a GR Mk 1, showing extent of natural metal panelling behind the jetpipes. Note contrast in metallic hues, that immediately below the stabilisers having a distinctly brownish tinge. RBF tag is red and white striped.
Below: Jaguar's twin tailpipes. RAF

aircraft have all been retrofitted with the Adour 104 (RT.172-26), offering a thrust of 4195lb on each powerplant, with 8720lb on reheat; Rolls-Royce/Turboméca have further developed the Adour, to -58 and -68 versions, for even greater output, although the latter requires changes in the geometry of the tailpipes and is unlikely to be adopted by the RAF.

Right: Tailfin of Jaguar GR Mk 1, showing the ECM fairing.
Below: Rear tip of fuselage, showing parachute brake cone and fuel dump.
Bottom: Fin of Jaguar T Mk 2; the ECM fairing is not fitted to two-seaters.
Opposite page, top: Starboard lower fin area of a No 41 Sqn GR Mk 1. This aircraft had just landed when it was photographed, hence the jettisoned parabrake fairing. Note attachment hook.
Opposite page, bottom: Port stabiliser of T Mk 2 (GR Mk 1 is similar), with the distinctive 'kink' in the trailing edge clearly visible. Note squared-off tip.

M
XII

NO STEP
NO STEP

NO STEP
NO STEP
WELD ON
WELD ON
NO STEP
XX829

NO STEP

Opposite page, top: Starboard oblique view of a GR Mk 1 showing upper wing camouflage and position of roundel. Other noteworthy points are the black antenna panel at the forward wing root and the sharp boundary and darker green appearance across the bulge over the primary heat exchanger.
Opposite page, middle: Upper fuselage and wing surface detail of a T Mk 2, showing clearly the scoop and outlets for the heat exchanger aft. Note that the entire wing trailing edge is occupied by double-slotted flaps, shown here drooped (in contrast to the previous photo); roll is achieved via spoilers forward of the outboard flaps.
Opposite page, bottom: Flap detail, starboard wing (GR Mk 1).
Top: Uppersurface view of Jaguar trainer, showing anti-collision light.
Above: Starboard outer wing surface, T Mk 2, with leading-edge slat fully extended; the photo also shows the shape and extent of the wing fence. Rounded wingtip contrasts with straight edges of prototype aircraft.

UNDERCARRIAGE

Below: Rear starboard view of nosewheel leg, Jaguar GR Mk 1. General finish of leg is glossy Light Aircraft Grey; inside surfaces of doors are yellowish zinc chromate primer. Note secondary forward door nestling behind the larger unit and landing light mountings above.
Opposite page, top left: No 54 Sqn GR Mk 1 nosewheel gear, showing shape of forward door; the latter is finished in the squadron colours of blue and yellow.
Opposite page, top right: Rear view of nosewheel undercarriage of the same machine as that shown in the previous photo. Production Jaguars show very different nosegear arrangements from those adopted on prototype aircraft: a single wheel 'yoke' and a total of four doors instead of two.
Opposite page, bottom left: Detail of nose undercarriage bay. General finish of interior and insides of doors shown here is yellowish primer.
Opposite page, bottom right: Port side of nosewheel, GR Mk 1.

REFUELING PRESSURE
NOT TO EXCEED 75 P S I
WITH DROP TANK FITTED
NOT TO EXCEED 25 P S I

Opposite page, top: Upper part of starboard undercarriage gear. External finish of leg is glossy Light Aircraft Grey.

Opposite page, bottom: Starboard main wheels of the same aircraft, a GR Mk 1. Note the retraction stay joining the inner door to the leg.

Above: Port main undercarriage gear, viewed from forward. The Jaguar's undercarriage is particularly complex, principally because the aircraft has a high-mounted 'shoulder' wing, which necessitates stowing the main wheels within the fuselage and the 'splayed' configuration demanded by this arrangement in order to provide sufficient track. The aircraft was also designed to operate from semi-prepared airstrips, which in turn required either large-diameter wheels (for which there was inadequate accommodation within the fuselage) or alternatively twin wheels (which were hence adopted). The main legs can absorb a descent rate of about 11.5ft/sec, and with the braking parachute deployed the stopping distance is reputed to be as little as 1600ft. Nosewheel steering is provided, making the aircraft very manoeuvrable on the ground, and pilots are reported to have commented favourably on the smooth taxying characteristics, even over rough, semi-prepared surfaces. Much publicised, though little practised, have been take-offs and landings from roads and motorways, for which the Jaguar's high ground clearance, lever-type undercarriage dampers and virtual STOL characteristics would appear to be ideally suited.

Below: Port main undercarriage leg from side-on; lower surfaces of external wing-mounted fuel tank are visible at the top of the photograph.
Opposite page, top: Starboard main undercarriage bay is yellow zinc chromate primer, with fittings in black, natural metal and Light Aircraft Grey. Message on lower door reads 'When rod disconnected door must be removed' and refers to the retraction jack, the lower hinge of which is just visible.
Opposite page, bottom: Internal details of port main bay are similar to starboard bay though not identical. The forward (large) doors of each main undercarriage unit are frequently to be seen open when the aircraft is parked on the flight line, or just the lower unit – or both may be closed. The rear nosewheel doors may similarly be either open or closed. Needless to say, the ground-retractable lower main doors are favourite locations for 'unofficial' messages, 'zapping' and so forth, details of which will not be disclosed!

COCKPIT

Below left: Jaguar GR Mk 1 cockpit canopy in raised position: note actuator struts at far left, behind the seat, twin rear-view mirrors along forward frame and guide lugs across lower frame of windscreen.

Below right: Close-up of emergency canopy release: this is the port-side handle but that on the starboard side is identical. Panels are yellow and lettering etc black.

Bottom: Personal markings as applied to No 54 Sqn's XX731/'GK', June 1983. Lettering is in white. Warning triangle is standard red and white, and crew entry ladder at far right is in this instance drab. Sealing strips for glazing are reddish-brown.

Opposite page, top: Instrument panel of an early production Jaguar GR Mk 1 (No 6 Sqn, RAF Lossiemouth, mid-1970s). General finish is matt dark grey. *Bob Jones Collection*

Opposite page, bottom: Port side console and seat detail of the same aircraft, with engine throttles prominent. *Bob Jones Collection*

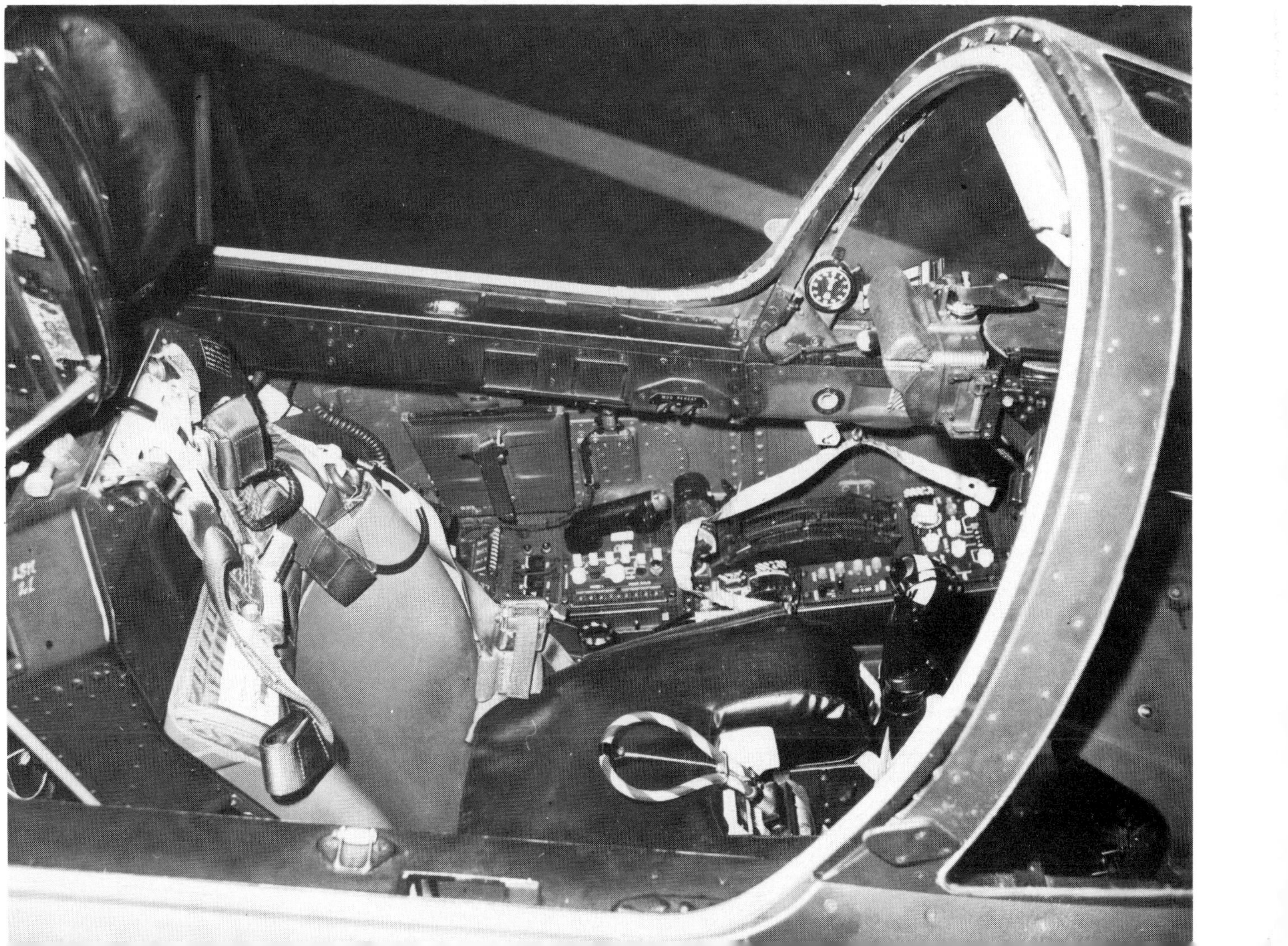

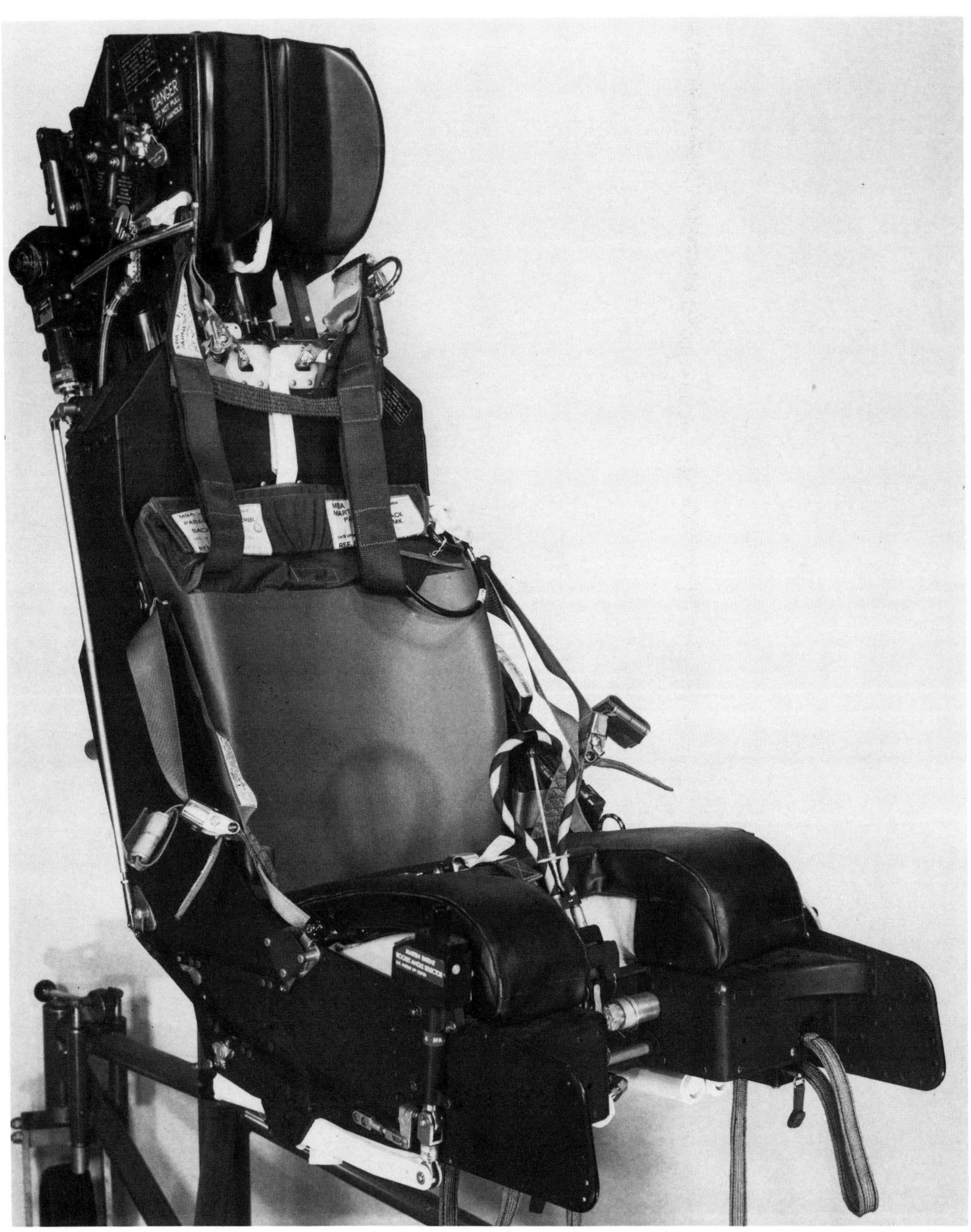

Above and opposite page: The Martin-Baker Mk 9B is the standard ejection seat fitted to the aircraft depicted in this booklet. The seat was developed in the late 1960s and early 1970s and showed several innovations and improvements over existing designs, in particular a new gas-operated firing system activated by means of a single handle attached to the seat pan and clearly evident in the photos. In order to facilitate escape, the pilot pulls the firing handle which withdraws a sear from a breech unit beneath the seat; the gas so generated retracts the pilot's harness to restrain him in the correct posture for ejection and also rotates a shaft at the top of the seat frame which operates the ejection gun and thus fires the seat. The pipe along which the gas travels can be seen

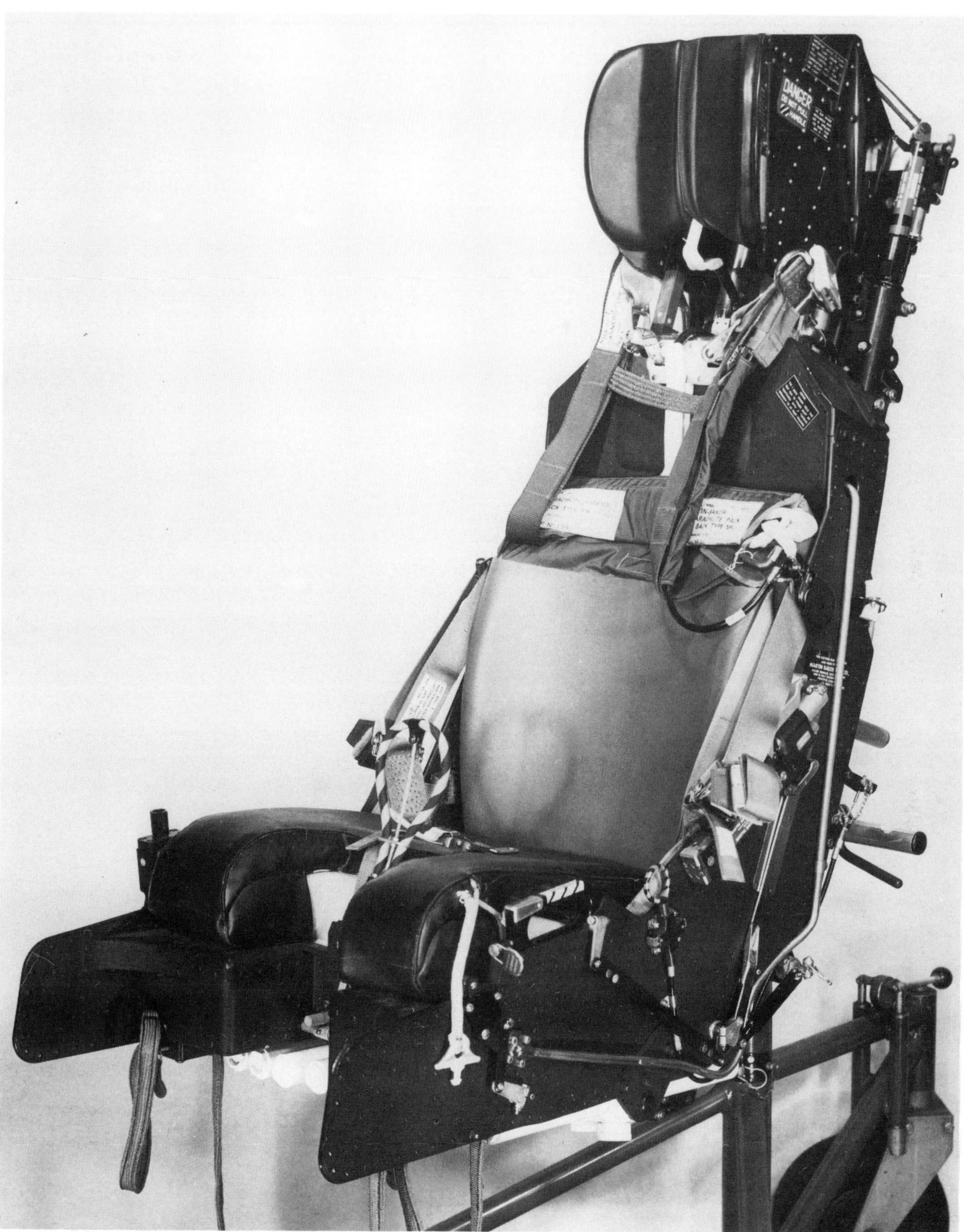

in the right-hand photo emerging from beneath the pan and then running up the rear structure; the ejection gun is fitted behind the padded headrest and the sear withdrawal unit which activates it is the tube-like fitting visible at the side of the headrest. The pilot's parachute is fitted as a combination backrest, the drogue chute for the seat being stowed in the headrest. Beneath the seat pan is the rocket pack, comprising a row of 1in combustion tubes with downward-pointing nozzles at the rear. Note that leg restraints are fitted, though not arm restraints as in the later Mk 10 seat. From a pilot's point of view, the Mk 9 represented a significant improvement in standards of comfort, with considerably more padding than in previous designs.
Martin-Baker Aircraft Co Ltd

WEAPONS & STORES

Below: A July 1983 photograph of a No 226 OCU Jaguar T Mk 2 based at RAF Lossiemouth, showing the standard 264gal underwing tank. Note that the latter is completely camouflaged in Dark Sea Grey and Dark Green; the aircraft itself has its undersurfaces finished in Light Aircraft Grey. *Royal Air Force*
Middle: Aden cannon (30mm), port side, Jaguar GR Mk 1, showing shape of blast trough and arrangement of gas venting.
Bottom: Starboard cannon of the same aircraft; RBF tag hangs from intake blanking plate.
Opposite page, top: Port wing stores of No 54 Sqn GR Mk 1 XX722/'GF', June 1983, comprising the standard fuel tank (matt Dark Green) and a CBLS (Carrier, Bomb, Light Store, glossy Dark Green); the latter accommodates practice bombs in varying weights and quantities.
Opposite page, bottom: Detail of inboard wing pylon, starboard side. This view also shows the 'wrap-round' of the wing fence.

DANGER
EJECTOR
RELEASE
UNIT
DANGER
DANGER

Opposite page, top: Ground crew prepare to fit a 1000lb HE bomb to a No 31 Sqn Jaguar GR Mk 1 at Ramstein, July 1980. *Richard L Ward*

Opposite page, middle: A pair of 600lb cluster bombs fitted in tandem to the centreline pylon of XX721, a 54 Sqn Jaguar GR Mk 1 at Lossiemouth, June 1974. The aircraft shows the original Jaguar scheme of Dark Sea Grey and Dark Green camouflage with Light Aircraft Grey undersurfaces. *Richard L Ward*

Opposite page, bottom: Jaguar International display aircraft, showing overwing Sidewinder installation giving the aircraft a dogfighting capability. Matra 550 Magic missiles can be carried both in this position and underwing. Outer pylon carries a dummy 600lb cluster bomb.

Top: View of a No 41 Sqn Jaguar GR Mk 1 showing not only the reconnaissance pod on the underfuselage station but also how the ground equipment ('Houchin') and

splitter box is connected. The main function of this equipment is to 'warm up' the aircraft's navigation systems.

Above: The reconnaissance pod from the starboard side. When activated, the lower centrebody of the pod rotates to reveal three Vinten F59 cameras (one forward-looking) in the forward drum and two further F95 cameras (high-oblique, across-track) for low-level or one F126 camera for high- or medium-altitude work in the rear drum. Infra-red linescan equipment is fitted aft.

SCALE COLOUR PLANS

SEPECAT JAGUAR GR Mk 1, No 54 SQN, RAF COLTISHALL, JULY 1983

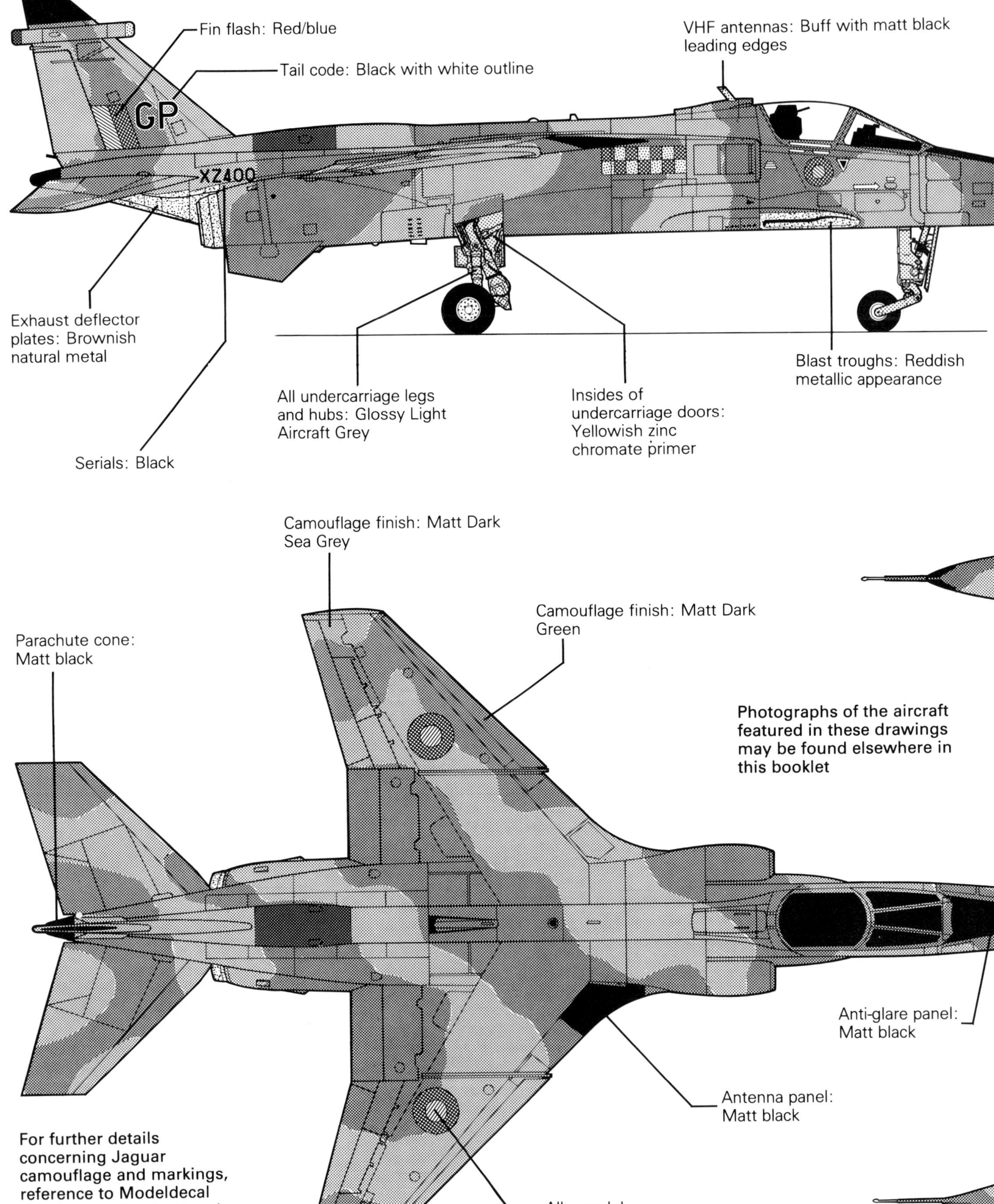

For further details concerning Jaguar camouflage and markings, reference to Modeldecal sets 29, 30, 32, 38, 43 and 46 is recommended

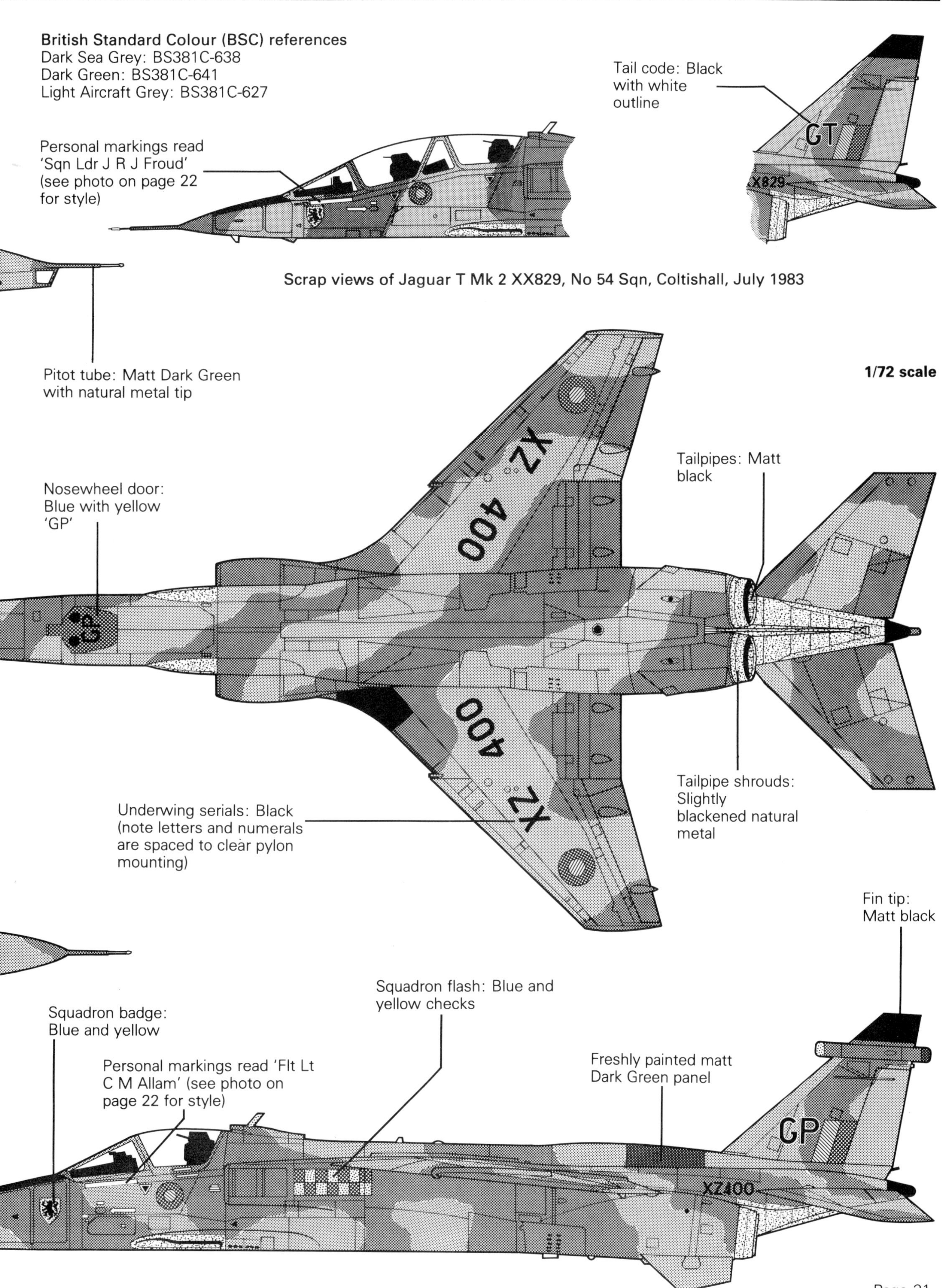

Scrap views of Jaguar T Mk 2 XX829, No 54 Sqn, Coltishall, July 1983

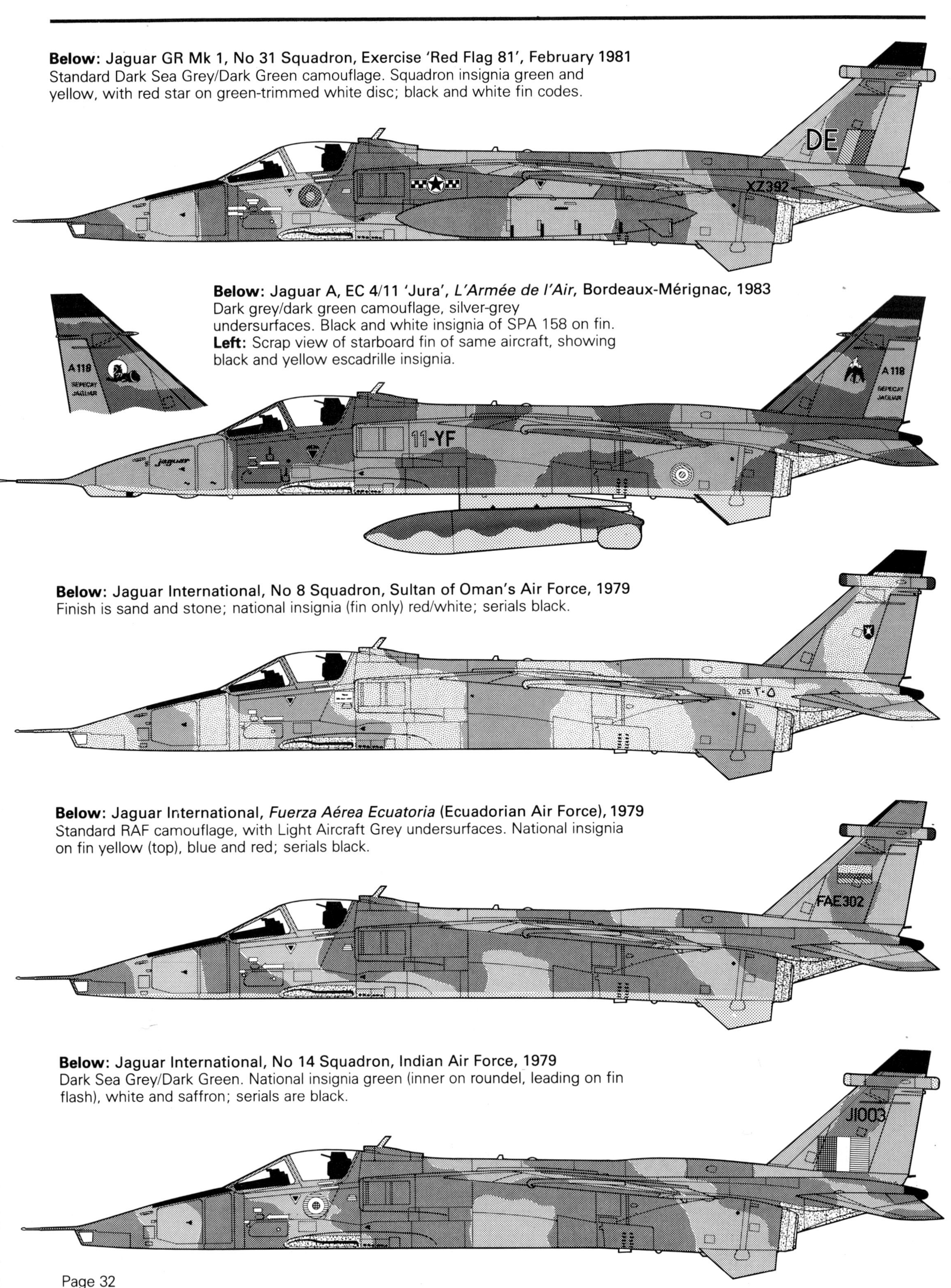

Below: Jaguar GR Mk 1, No 31 Squadron, Exercise 'Red Flag 81', February 1981
Standard Dark Sea Grey/Dark Green camouflage. Squadron insignia green and
yellow, with red star on green-trimmed white disc; black and white fin codes.

Below: Jaguar A, EC 4/11 'Jura', *L'Armée de l'Air*, Bordeaux-Mérignac, 1983
Dark grey/dark green camouflage, silver-grey
undersurfaces. Black and white insignia of SPA 158 on fin.
Left: Scrap view of starboard fin of same aircraft, showing
black and yellow escadrille insignia.

Below: Jaguar International, No 8 Squadron, Sultan of Oman's Air Force, 1979
Finish is sand and stone; national insignia (fin only) red/white; serials black.

Below: Jaguar International, *Fuerza Aérea Ecuatoria* (Ecuadorian Air Force), 1979
Standard RAF camouflage, with Light Aircraft Grey undersurfaces. National insignia
on fin yellow (top), blue and red; serials black.

Below: Jaguar International, No 14 Squadron, Indian Air Force, 1979
Dark Sea Grey/Dark Green. National insignia green (inner on roundel, leading on fin
flash), white and saffron; serials are black.